UNNATURAL DISASTERS

CHEMICAL CATASTROPHES

By Danielle Haynes

Gareth Stevens
PUBLISHING

Please visit our website, www.garethstevens.com. For a free color catalog of all our high-quality books, call toll free 1-800-542-2595 or fax 1-877-542-2596.

Cataloging-in-Publication Data
Names: Haynes, Danielle.
Title: Chemical catastrophes / Danielle Haynes.
Description: New York : Gareth Stevens Publishing, 2018. | Series: Unnatural disasters | Includes index.
Identifiers: ISBN 9781538204351 (pbk.) | ISBN 9781538204184 (library bound) | ISBN 9781538204177 (6 pack)
Subjects: LCSH: Chemical spills–History–20th century–Juvenile literature. | Chemicals--Accidents–History–20th century–Juvenile literature. | Chemical warfare–Juvenile literature.
Classification: LCC TP150.A23 H39 2018 | DDC 363.11'09–dc23

First Edition

Published in 2018 by
Gareth Stevens Publishing
111 East 14th Street, Suite 349
New York, NY 10003

Copyright © 2018 Gareth Stevens Publishing

Designer: Sam DeMartin
Editor: Joan Stoltman

Photo credits: Cover, p. 1 Peter Turnley/Corbis Historical/Getty Images; p. 5 Ververidis Vasilis/Shutterstock.com; p. 7 (pest control) janews/Shutterstock.com; p. 7 (DDT sprayer) PongMoji/Shutterstock.com; p. 8 (book) courtesy of the Library of Congress; p. 8 (Carson) Luis Fernández García/Wikimedia Commons; p. 9 Serjio/Shutterstock.com; p. 10 Everett Historical/Shutterstock.com; p. 11 Angela Ostafichuk/Shutterstock.com; p. 12 AFP/AFP/Getty Images; p. 13 (danger sign) Kim Britten/Shutterstock.com; p. 13 (Vietnam) Harvepino/Shutterstock.com; p. 14 Bruno Vincent/Getty Images News/Getty Images; p. 15 Francois LOCHON/Gamma-Rapho/Getty Images; p. 16 The Asahi Shimbun/The Asahi Shimbun/Getty Images; p. 17 Ventin/Shutterstock.com; p. 18 Sementer/Shutterstock.com; p. 19 Suttha Burawonk/Shutterstock.com; p. 20 goccedicolore.it/Shutterstock.com; p. 21 MikeDotta/Shutterstock.com; p. 23 courtesy of NASA; pp. 24, 26, 27 China Photos/Getty Images News/Getty Images; p. 25 Bardocz Peter/Shutterstock.com; p. 29 paintings/Shutterstock.com.

All rights reserved. No part of this book may be reproduced in any form without permission in writing from the publisher, except by a reviewer.

Printed in the United States of America

CPSIA compliance information: Batch #CS17GS: For further information contact Gareth Stevens, New York, New York at 1-800-542-2595.

CONTENTS

Defining the Problem 4
A Problematic Pesticide 6
Poison as a Weapon 10
Explosion in Italy 14
Deadly Waters in Japan 16
Toxic Mining in Montana 18
Air Pollution in Russia 22
Toxic Drinking Water in China 24
Be an Agent for Change! 28
Glossary 30
For More Information 31
Index 32

Words in the glossary appear in **bold** type the first time they are used in the text.

DEFINING THE PROBLEM

Help! There are chemicals all around us! Actually, it's not that scary. Every bit of matter is made up of chemicals, including ourselves! These chemicals exist by themselves as elements or can combine together. For example, water is a combination of the elements hydrogen and oxygen. Some of these natural elements and compounds can be toxic to humans.

Humans have also made many toxic materials over the years by tinkering with elements.

Whether created in nature or by humans, many of these dangers weren't immediately understood. Some harmful chemicals were even used in building, farming, and more. Sadly, the harm of certain chemicals was even ignored at several points in history! Explosions or poor maintenance at plants, mines, and factories can also expose people to large quantities of harmful materials.

WHAT IS AN ECO-ACTIVIST?

An eco-activist is someone who spends time actively working to protect the **environment**, fight against pollution, and save natural resources. Eco-activists pursue these goals in several ways:

- they **lobby** politicians to pass environmentally friendly laws
- they protest practices that are damaging to the environment, animals, or humans
- they organize boycotts, or bans on purchasing goods or services, from companies that harm the environment
- they educate the public about the environment

4

LASTING EFFECT

In the United States, the Environmental Protection Agency (EPA) regulates what companies can expose the environment and people to. They also manage cleanups of explosions, accidents, and **abuse** of land, air, and water.

In 2012, these protesters in Greece were fighting mining in Stratoni, Greece, to protect people and the environment.

A PROBLEMATIC PESTICIDE

DDT is one of the world's most well-known pesticides, or pest-killing chemicals. It was created in 1874, but its ability to kill insects wasn't discovered until the 1930s. In the 1940s, it was so widely accepted that some countries, including the United States, applied it to soldiers, **refugees,** and prisoners during World War II (1939-1945) to protect them from deadly bug bites. Back in the United States, the land around homes across the country was sprayed with the so-called miracle chemical.

But in the late 1950s, researchers discovered DDT was making people sick. Even people who had only been exposed to the chemical by eating crops and foods treated with DDT were getting sick! In 1972, the EPA banned the use of DDT except in emergencies.

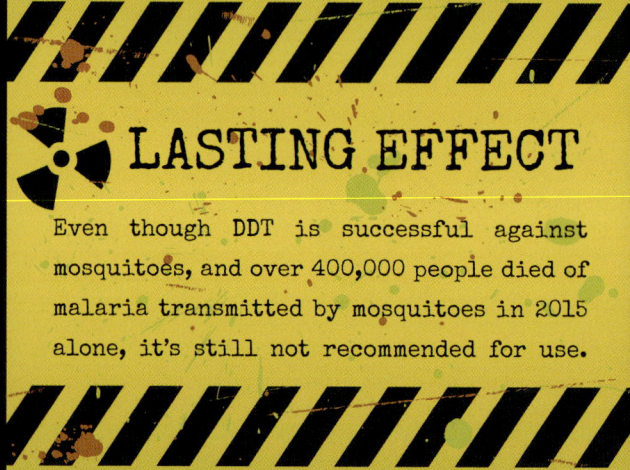

LASTING EFFECT

Even though DDT is successful against mosquitoes, and over 400,000 people died of malaria transmitted by mosquitoes in 2015 alone, it's still not recommended for use.

Some areas in the world receive special permission from the World Health Organization to spray DDT because of a disease outbreak. In these cases, the risks of DDT are considered less serious because there is such a high chance of death without it.

FAST FACTS ON DDT USE

- **poison:** DDT
- **what happened:** hundreds of thousands of people worldwide were dying from lice and mosquito bites that spread deadly diseases such as typhus and malaria, so DDT was sprayed on people, crops, and animals to kill insects carrying diseases
- **when used:** invented in 1874; widely used by the 1940s
- **where used:** worldwide
- **symptoms:** coughing, vomiting, tremors, **seizures**
- **still unknown:** research connecting DDT to **cancer** is still ongoing

PEST CONTROL

The dangers of DDT were most famously written about by American scientist and author Rachel Carson. Her 1962 book *Silent Spring* warned of the dangers of using synthetic, or man-made, pesticides, DDT in particular. Carson's work inspired a generation of eco-activists throughout the world.

Rachel Carson

The publishing of *Silent Spring* led to swift law changes in Sweden, Finland, and Great Britain, but France, Germany, and the Netherlands protected the companies that made the chemicals Carson wrote about.

INSECTICIDE EXPOSURE IN MISSISSIPPI

For nearly a decade, pest control workers sprayed an insecticide, or insect-killing chemical, inside hundreds of homes and businesses, even though it was only approved for outdoor use, and got many people sick.

- **poison:** methyl parathion
- **when:** from around 1986 to around 1996
- **where:** Jackson County, Mississippi
- **symptoms:** breathing problems, nosebleeds, vomiting, digestive problems, nerve problems, mental health issues
- **cleanup cost:** estimated $69 to $100 million

The EPA's ban on DDT was one of its first acts as an official government organization. This ban aimed to protect people, but also ended up saving an **endangered species**! The bald eagle—our national bird—was nearly extinct, with only 487 nesting pairs existing in 1963. Since the ban, the bald eagle has flourished, and about 10,000 nesting pairs exist throughout the country today!

LASTING EFFECT

The EPA works with the president and Congress to write and enforce laws in the United States and get funding. In 2017, the EPA spent nearly $140 million on cleanup projects across America!

POISON AS A WEAPON

"Agent Orange" was the nickname given to a chemical mixture used during the Vietnam War (1954-1975). The government in South Vietnam gave permission to the US Army to spray Agent Orange over about 10 percent of their country. The hope was that the chemical mixture would kill the trees their enemies hid in and the crops they ate.

The US Army sprayed Agent Orange and other chemical mixtures over South Vietnam for over a decade during the Vietnam War.

Chemical mixtures nicknamed Agents White, Pink, Purple, Green, and Blue—together known as the Rainbow Herbicides, or plant killers—were also dumped over South Vietnam. Using these chemicals was part of the US military's support of the government of South Vietnam against a communist revolt. Unfortunately, the world soon found out that Agent Orange didn't just damage plants.

LASTING EFFECT

Agent Orange exposure poisoned US soldiers and many innocent Vietnamese citizens. Anyone who even handled the chemical mixture was affected! Wherever it was sprayed, it seeped into the ground, entered the water, and contaminated, or polluted, the entire food chain.

AGENT ORANGE FAST FACTS

- **poison:** Agent Orange, which includes the deadly chemical TCDD
- **what happened:** to kill plants used by enemies for protection and food, 12.1 million gallons (46 million L) was sprayed from the air during 20,000 flights
- **land affected:** over 5 million acres (2 million ha), with 34 percent of areas sprayed more than once
- **crops affected:** nearly 500,000 acres (202,000 million ha)
- **symptoms:** muscle problems, **birth defects**, nerve issues and illnesses, and a variety of cancers

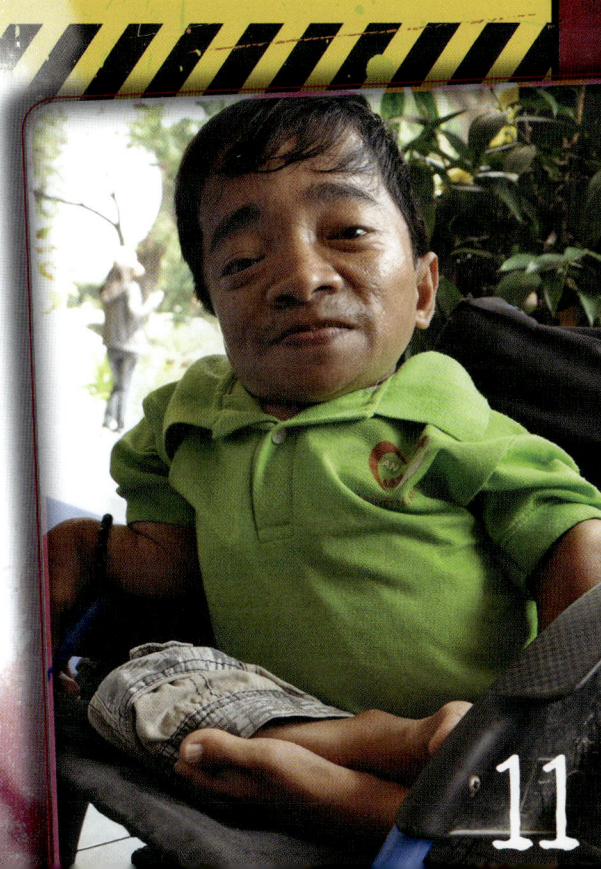

Vietnamese officials report that Agent Orange killed or injured 400,000 people at the time of its use. Sadly, the effects of Agent Orange didn't limit themselves to one generation. Babies born to people poisoned by the chemical mixture also often had serious physical defects. Missing limbs were a common birth defect caused by Agent Orange. In the years that followed, more than 2 million people would show signs of TCDD exposure.

Exposure to Agent Orange caused many severe birth defects in the generation after the war. Kids are still born in Vietnam with defects caused by Agent Orange because the cleanup isn't done yet, so exposure continues.

LASTING EFFECT

In 1979, 2.4 million **veterans** sued the companies that created Agent Orange and were awarded $240 million, around $100 per soldier. No affected Vietnamese citizens have been awarded money.

Vietnam

Decades after the war ended, the United States and Vietnam agreed to clean up areas that still had high concentrations of Agent Orange in the soil. The United States estimates it will spend about $43 million to dig up the contaminated soil and treat it.

REDSTONE ARSENAL: ANOTHER NIGHTMARE CAUSED BY WEAPONS

A wide array of killer chemicals was used as weapons by all sides in World War II (1939–1945). After the war, the United States collected over 1 million unused chemical weapons from Germany, Japan, and Great Britain, and buried them outside Huntsville, Alabama, until 1949. Unfortunately, the weapons leaked throughout the 38,000-acre (15,380 ha) dump site. The weapons are still underground today, and groundwater has spread the poisons beyond the dump site.

13

EXPLOSION IN ITALY

In 1976, another group of people were exposed to the same dangerous chemical found in Agent Orange, TCDD. An explosion at a chemical plant in Italy released a toxic cloud of the chemical. The cloud drifted over 11 communities filled with residents, poisoning a 5.8-square-mile (15 sq km) area. The town of Seveso was most severely affected.

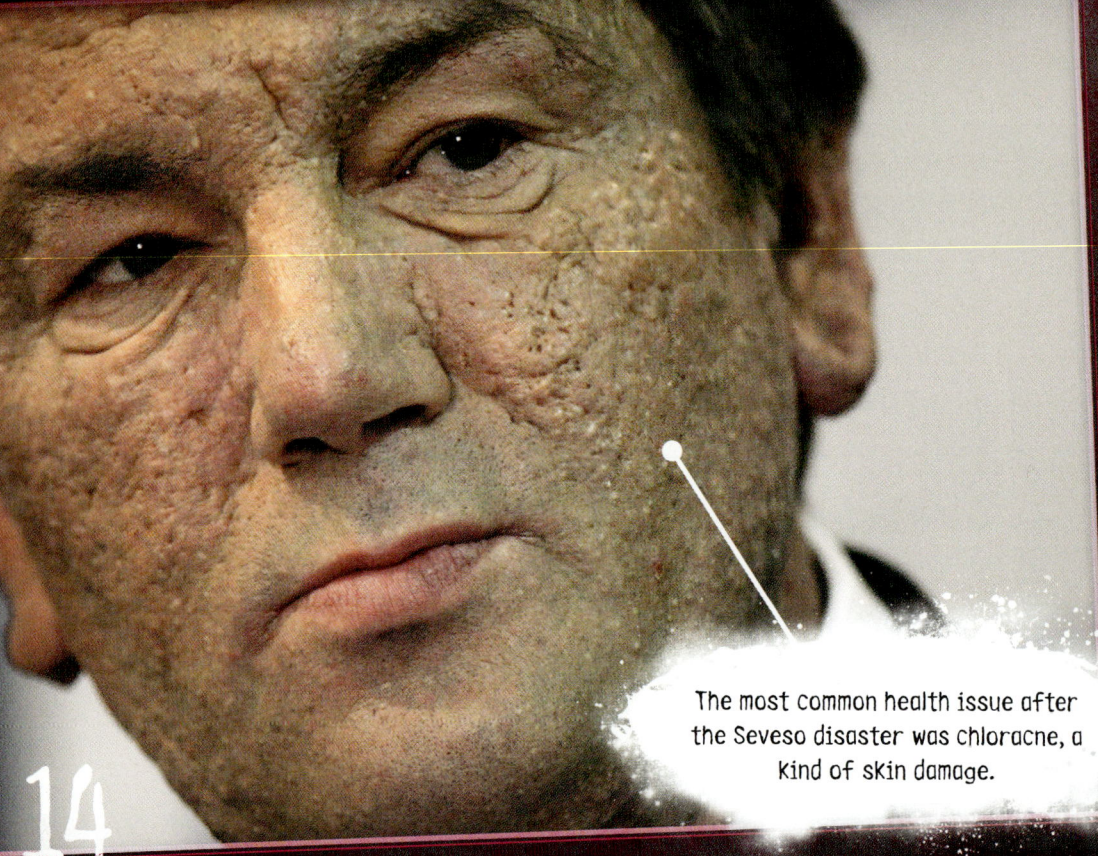

The most common health issue after the Seveso disaster was chloracne, a kind of skin damage.

LASTING EFFECT

The Seveso disaster scared Europe into action. A law was named after it in 1982 to regulate the safety of facilities where dangerous materials are created and stored throughout Europe.

People already knew by 1976 that TCDD was probably one of the most toxic man-made chemicals ever, but the effect on the health of the people exposed in the explosion showed up slowly. To clean up the area affected by the explosion, the top layer of soil was removed from the land. Then, they made the area into Seveso Oak Forest Park, a TCDD-free public park.

FAST FACTS: THE SEVESO DISASTER

- **poison:** TCDD
- **what happened:** TCDD, a by-product, or leftover, of some chemical or metal processing, was sprayed out in a plant explosion
- **when:** July 10, 1976
- **where:** multiple towns 12 miles (19 km) north of Milan, Italy
- **people affected:** 37,000 people (17,000 in Seveso alone)
- **symptoms:** skin damage, liver issues, nerve and reproductive problems

DEADLY WATERS IN JAPAN

In the early 1950s, doctors in Minamata, Japan, saw that residents were suffering from terrible medical problems. The local animals were acting strange, too, with birds crashing into the ground and cats shaking violently. It took until 1959 to prove people and animals in the area were being poisoned by a local chemical company that was dumping a metal called mercury into the water. The local fish were absorbing the mercury, then being eaten by humans, birds, cats, and other fish.

Finding the cause, however, didn't stop the company, and they continued dumping for nearly a decade into a nearby 1.5-square-mile (3.9 sq km) body of water.

a close-up of mercury

The company and the Japanese government removed some of the mercury from the sea, but couldn't clean it all. The part of the seafloor they couldn't clean up was covered up using steel and cement.

FAST FACTS: THE MINAMATA DISASTER

- **poison:** methylmercury, a kind of mercury
- **what happened:** a successful chemical factory dumped 27 tons (24.5 mt) of waste mercury mixtures into Minamata Bay
- **when:** 1932 through 1968
- **where:** Minamata and Minamata Bay, Japan
- **people affected:** at least 2,200 killed; 30,000 to 40,000 made ill
- **symptoms:** problems with speech, sight, hearing, movement, and muscles

LASTING EFFECT

An international treaty named after the disaster was created in 2013 to ban mercury mining, develop safe ways to store and dispose of waste materials with mercury, and control the amount of mercury released into the environment. Only 35 countries have signed it.

17

TOXIC MINING IN MONTANA

Asbestos is the name for several minerals that have been used heavily in manufacturing and building around the world since the Industrial Revolution. It's been used in **insulation**, car brakes, cement, ovens, engines, fireproofing, pipes, roads, roofing, flooring, and more. As early as the 1930s, doctors knew asbestos caused lung illness in humans, but it continued to be in high demand into the 1970s.

A mineral called vermiculite in a mine near the town of Libby, Montana, was contaminated with asbestos and sent the toxic material into the air, water, and land for nearly 7 decades. The mine finally closed in 1990. Even today, the EPA says people can still easily be exposed to the toxin in certain parts of Libby.

Asbestos fibers can get into the lungs, causing scars, damage, and cancers to form.

a close-up of an asbestos fiber

FAST FACTS: THE ASBESTOS POISONING OF LIBBY

- **poison:** asbestos, the common name for six similar minerals
- **what happened:** one of the most successful vermiculite mines in the world contaminated air and soil with asbestos during mining
- **when:** the early 1920s until 1990
- **where:** Libby, Montana
- **symptoms:** lung problems, lung cancers
- **people affected:** more than 200 killed, over 1,000 sick out of a total population of 2,600

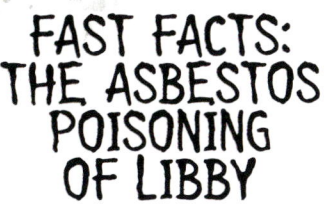

an x-ray showing lung cancer

LASTING EFFECT

The EPA took legal action on behalf of Libby residents because they had been lied to since the 1960s about the asbestos so the mine could keep making money. In 2009, the EPA declared a public health emergency for the first time ever. It was in Libby, Montana.

Asbestos isn't just a problem in Libby, Montana. Archaeologists have evidence that humans have been using the material since 4000 BC. At the height of its popularity, it was mined on every continent except Antarctica. In the 1970s, 25 countries mined close to 5.3 million tons (4.8 million mt) of asbestos per year, and 85 countries manufactured the raw material into products to sell.

The EPA tried to ban products containing asbestos in 1989, but failed. The last asbestos mine in the United States wasn't closed until 2002. Even more frightening, the use of asbestos is still not banned here, even though 50 other countries have banned it entirely. Companies that still use asbestos spend millions of dollars every year lobbying against laws that would ban asbestos.

MORE TERRIBLE MOMENTS IN ASBESTOS HISTORY

- In ancient Rome, asbestos miners breathed through cleaned animal organ tissue to filter the fibers out of the air!
- Henry Ward Johns, the man who made asbestos popular in construction, died at age 61 from asbestos exposure.
- Medical expenses for lung diseases, like hospital visits, medicines, and treatments, cost a lot. In 1908, insurance companies—the companies that pay medical expenses—throughout North America began charging asbestos workers more money, but covering fewer treatments.

roofing tiles

Today, construction workers who handle asbestos must wear protective clothing and use special equipment to safely remove it.

☢ LASTING EFFECT

Between 12,000 and 15,000 Americans and over 107,000 worldwide still die each year from illnesses caused by asbestos. Many third-world countries, or countries that are just beginning to grow their own industries, are embracing asbestos, so that number will likely rise.

AIR POLLUTION IN RUSSIA

Norilsk is a remote village only 1,400 miles (2,300 km) away from the North Pole. There aren't even roads or trains leading there! It may sound like a very private ski resort, but it's actually one of the top 10 worst ecological disaster locations in the world.

This Arctic mining town sits on top of huge mines that contain heavy metals used to make batteries, cell phones, cars, and more. The metals are mined and then smelted, or purified, through a process of heating and melting, which produces a poisonous smoke. That smoke is pumped outside, contaminating the air and soil, making the rain poisonous in a 138,000-square-mile (357,000 sq km) area, and killing all trees within 19 miles (31 km) of the town.

FAST FACTS: THE NORILSK AIR PROBLEM

- **poison:** sulfur dioxide and the metals cadmium, copper, lead, nickel, arsenic, selenium, and zinc, which are known as heavy metals
- **what happened:** 6 million tons (5.4 million mt) of heavy metals and sulfur dioxide released into the air yearly from factories from 1935 to present
- **where:** Norilsk, Russia
- **symptoms:** higher rates of lung and digestive diseases and cancers
- **people affected:** over 130,000 residents of Norilsk exposed daily

Smoke from the Norilsk Nickel mine can be seen from space.

LASTING EFFECT

The factories made $2 billion in profits in the first half of 2006, and there are enough metals for mining to continue for another 30 or more years. With possible profits of $120 billion in that time, it's unlikely these factories will become more environmentally friendly unless a new law requires them to.

TOXIC DRINKING WATER IN CHINA

In 2005, there were explosions at a government chemical plant in Jilin, China. The explosion dumped 100 tons (91 mt) of toxic chemicals into the Songhua River. Over several weeks, the chemicals traveled down the river all the way into Russia.

FAST FACTS: CHEMICAL PLANT EXPLOSIONS IN JILIN, CHINA

- **poison:** benzene, aniline, nitrobenzene

- **how:** explosions in a factory that processed fuels into various products, including chemicals used for making plastics

- **when:** November 13, 2005

- **where:** Jilin, Harbin, Jiamusi, and other Chinese towns; Khabarovsk, Russia

- **symptoms:** lung and heart issues, cancers, and more

- **people affected:** 37 million exposed in northeastern China; 7 million exposed in Russia

- **area:** the entire Songhua River plus groundwater within 0.6 mile (1 km) of the river and wells within 1.3 miles (2 km)

Nearly 2 weeks passed before the Chinese government told the public. At first, they lied and said they were performing maintenance work on water supply pipes. Rumors quickly spread that an earthquake was coming and the pipes were being strengthened, and panic spread. The government was forced to tell the truth about the spill, but since they'd denied it for 11 days, a lot of damage had already been done. Many people, including the 4 million residents of Harbin, a city downriver from Jilin, were already poisoned from drinking the water.

LASTING EFFECT

Some of the chemicals spilled in the Jilin disaster were heavier than water and sank into the sediment. But Chinese scientists only measured chemicals in the surface water, resulting in much less scary—and less exact—measurements.

Massive amounts of deadly chemicals traveled hundreds of miles from China to Russia.

Unfortunately, the story gets worse. The factory that exploded in 2005 was one of many plants and factories built along the Songhua River during the 1950s. These facilities weren't ever improved with systems to stop or lessen environmental pollution. In 1999, 6 years before the Jilin explosion, research showed that the drinking water from the Songhua River was too polluted to consume. After the explosion, activists accused a drug company in Harbin of dumping toxins into the river for years.

Contaminated wells and rivers are often the only local water in villages. In 2011, China announced it would spend $5.5 billion over a decade to prevent and treat groundwater poisoning by heavy metals, man-made chemicals, and natural poisons.

LASTING EFFECT

A United Nations team tried to investigate the Jilin explosion, but wasn't allowed to. Since the only water tests were performed by the Chinese government, no one really knows what happened, how much the environment was polluted, or what the lasting effects will be.

Hopefully, this water isn't contaminated, and this child is safe. But since so much of the water in China is contaminated, the odds aren't good!

CHINA'S WATER PROBLEM

- about 70 percent of Chinese citizens drink water from underground sources
- around 90 percent of China's shallow groundwater is polluted
- nearly 40 percent of that shallow groundwater is so badly polluted that there are no existing processes, filters, or methods to make it safe enough to drink
- almost 190 million Chinese people fall ill every year because of water pollution
- around 60,000 Chinese people die every year because of contaminated water

BE AN AGENT FOR CHANGE!

START BEING AN ECO-ACTIVIST NOW!

- Write letters to local politicians, like your state governor or senator, in support of environmental protection laws.
- Contact companies that damage the environment, and urge them to change their practices.
- Join the environmental awareness club at your school, or start your own!
- Urge your family, neighbors, friends, and school to recycle.
- Reduce power usage by turning off lights when you leave a room.
- Conserve water by taking quick showers.

Whether a toxin is man-made, like DDT, or occurs naturally, like asbestos, so many substances have the power to damage, hurt, poison, and kill. Industrial accidents and mistakes are often what make the headlines for environmental issues. But common chemicals, like those found in cleaning supplies and car exhaust, affect the delicate environment, too.

When toxins get into a body of water, animals, plants, and people can be poisoned, and entire ecosystems can be thrown out of balance. When certain kinds of gases and matter get into Earth's atmosphere, the layer of gases that surrounds the planet gets damaged, causing **climate change**. Learning about disasters of the past can help you lead the world into a future where Earth is cared for, not harmed!

TIMELINE OF DISASTERS

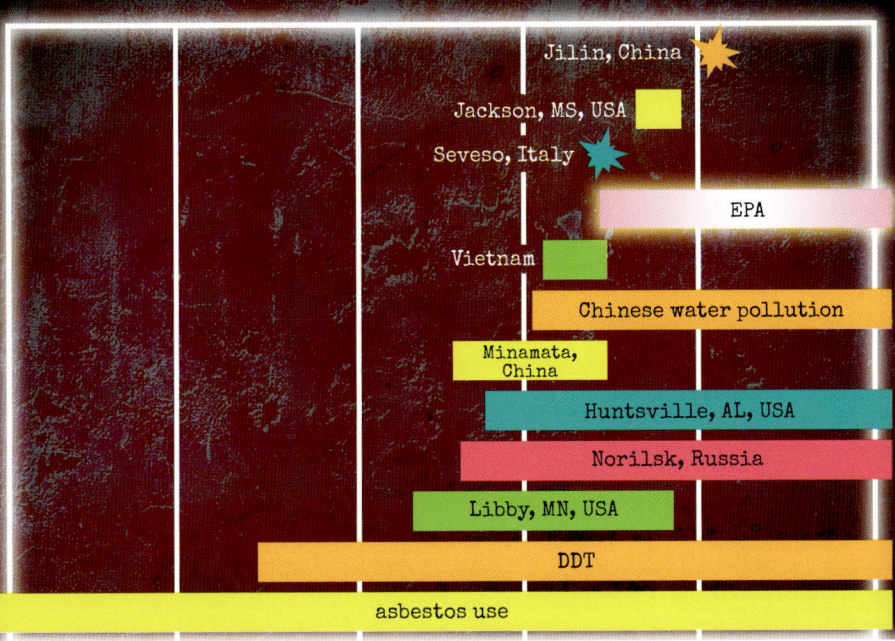

LASTING EFFECT

Since the beginning of the Industrial Revolution, many decades of people and companies abusing the land, water, and air have passed. The work to fix this damage needs to be a priority all around the world. Although some countries have started to pass laws protecting Earth, there is still much work to do.

GLOSSARY

abuse: a misuse of power that is often illegal

birth defect: a physical or chemical problem that exists at birth and is either passed down from the parents or caused by exposure to a toxin

cancer: a disease caused by the uncontrolled growth of cells in the body

climate change: long-term change in Earth's climate, caused partly by human activities such as burning oil and natural gas

endangered species: a kind of animal that is in danger of dying out

environment: the natural world in which a plant or animal lives

insulation: a material that surrounds something to prevent heat, electricity, or sound from passing through

lobby: to carry out activities with the goal of influencing a politician about a policy

refugee: someone who is seeking a safe place to live, especially during a time of war

seizure: a sudden attack to the body that is caused by issues in the brain

symptom: a sign that shows someone is sick

veteran: a retired armed forces member

FOR MORE INFORMATION

BOOKS

Fabiny, Sarah. *Who Was Rachel Carson?* New York, NY: Grosset & Dunlap, 2014.

Hollar, Sherman. *Poisoning Planet Earth: Pollution and Other Environmental Hazards.* New York, NY: Britannica Educational Publishing, 2012.

Kurlansky, Mark. *World Without Fish: How Could We Let this Happen?* New York, NY: Workman Publishing, 2011.

Websites

Earth Day Network

earthday.org

Read more about efforts to protect the environment and this holiday celebrating the environment.

A Student's Guide to Global Climate Change

www3.epa.gov/climatechange/kids

Read about ways you can help fight climate change.

Publisher's note to educators and parents: Our editors have carefully reviewed these websites to ensure that they are suitable for students. Many websites change frequently, however, and we cannot guarantee that a site's future contents will continue to meet our high standards of quality and educational value. Be advised that students should be closely supervised whenever they access the Internet.

INDEX

Agent Orange 10, 11, 12, 13, 14
asbestos 18, 19, 20, 21, 28
birth defects 11, 12
cancer 7, 11, 18, 19, 22, 24
Carson, Rachel 8
chemical weapons 13
climate change 28
DDT 6, 7, 8, 9, 28
eco-activist 4, 8, 26, 28
EPA 5, 6, 9, 18, 19, 20
heavy metals 22, 26
Jilin, China 24, 25, 26
Libby, Montana 18, 19, 20
mercury 16, 17
methyl parathion 9
Minamata, Japan 16, 17
Minamata Bay 17
mines 4, 17, 18, 19, 20, 22, 23
Norilsk, Russia 22
pesticides 6, 8
Seveso, Italy 14, 15
Silent Spring 8
Songhua River 24, 26
TCDD 11, 12, 14, 15
vermiculite 18, 19
Vietnam 10, 11, 12, 13